THE
AUDIENCE
REVOLUTION

The Smarter Way to Build a
Business, Make a Difference,
and Change the World

DANNY INY
Best-Selling Author of *Engagement from Scratch!*

THE AUDIENCE REVOLUTION
The Smarter Way to Build a Business, Make a Difference, and Change the World

by Danny Iny

Any Other Questions?

If you have any questions that haven't been answered here, you're welcome to contact the author via Firepole Marketing. Contact information is at http://www.firepolemarketing.com/contact-us

ISBN: 1508985596

ISBN 13: 978-1508985594

This book is dedicated to the wonderful people that work with me at Firepole Marketing.

If I am the face of Firepole Marketing, then you are its hands, legs, and most importantly, its heart. Thank you all for beating with such passion.

(Meet the whole team at firepolemarketing.com/our-team)

Contents

THE AUDIENCE REVOLUTION

The Smarter Way to Build a Business, Make a Difference, and Change the World

DANNY INY

Best-Selling Author of *Engagement from Scratch!*

Welcome to the Audience Revolution!

Failure is only failure if it happens in the last chapter. Otherwise, it's a plot twist.

This book is the result of a number of plot twists in my own journey as an entrepreneur, that led me to a startling and profound insight. At first it felt strange, and counter-intuitive. As I explored the idea further, I became more and more enthralled by its elegant simplicity, to the point where now I don't understand how I ever thought anything else could be true.

Over the last few years, my business has grown by leaps and bounds. After my last "plot twist" I had less than nothing: a failed business, and a quarter of a million dollars in personal debt. Now, just a few years later, my company generates multiple-seven-figures in annual revenue and employs almost twenty people. We do it all by serving thousands of customers and touching the lives of hundreds of thousands of people, who feel similarly driven to leverage their knowledge and expertise for the benefit of those around them. They are bloggers, authors, coaches, consultants, freelancers, speakers, and changemakers, and we've done so well because we help them do well, and make the world a better place for us all.

Think about that for a moment; we do well by helping *them* do well. How different is that from the social responsibility agendas of most corporations, who contribute only so they can offset their own societal and environmental damage? For a long time, that was the world that we lived in; there was always a choice to be made between doing what we knew to be right, in line with our values, and good for the world, versus the smart business decision that would make us more money.

There was a time when that was a real choice that entrepreneurs had to struggle with. But that time is being swept away by the Audience Revolution, and it's giving way to a new paradigm of income through impact. The most successful people and businesses in the modern age achieve their results by making the world a better place. And sure, you can still make money by screwing people over, but not sustainably, or for very long. Whether that means months, years, or decades depends on the scale at which you're operating, but even decades are just a blink of an eye on a global scale.

The greatest impact creates the greatest success, and the best way to make that impact is by putting the Audience First. That's the core insight that drives the Audience Revolution. I will unpack it for you in this book, so that you can understand and apply it to create your own success — by making your own impact. Along the way I'll show you how this approach has been used by successful businesses from Netflix and Copyblogger, to celebrity consultants like Jim Collins and Scott Stratten, to best-selling authors like Seth Godin and Jeff Walker, to internationally renowned speakers like Randy Gage and Mitch Joel. Through their examples, you'll learn how you can apply this Audience First strategy to your own business, to get you better results faster, make you more profitable, and decrease your risk, all at the same time.

Now before we dive in too deeply, I want to make clear who this book is for — because while the principles shared here apply to almost every business in the world (with a few notable exceptions), I personally don't have the experience or expertise to guide each and every one of them. So while the concepts will likely apply to what you're doing, I'll focus specifically on the new entrepreneurship that is transcending geographic regions and national borders.

I'm talking about those same bloggers, authors, coaches, consultants, freelancers, speakers, and changemakers; anyone who has knowledge, expertise, or talent that can be valuable to someone somewhere, and who seeks to leverage the online world to reach those people and make their lives a little better. There are four main categories of businesses that will benefit tremendously from what I share in this book:

- **Selling Products** — The most popular products among the entrepreneurs that I train tend to be education products like e-books, membership sites, and online training course. But these ideas will apply just as effectively if you sell physical goods, or even software.

- **Selling Services** — I support many businesses that sell services, from coaching, to consulting, to freelancing, to writing, to design, and other niche and esoteric offers. If you sell a service, these ideas will apply to you.

- **Writing and Publishing** — Whether you write fiction or non-fiction, plan to self-publish or land a traditional book deal, want your work read on paper or exclusively in digital formats, the Audience Revolution is critical to your future success.

- **Speaking and Training** — This includes speaking at conferences, keynoting, doing training for major corporations, and also providing services to C-suite executives. If that's your bread and butter (or you want it to be), you need these ideas.

If your business falls into one (or more!) of these four categories, I promise that the ideas shared in these pages will have a transformative impact on the way you approach and think about your work.

Now, in the interest of full disclosure, there are also three special cases — categories of business that will not benefit much from these ideas. They are:

- **Commodities** — If you're selling something that is exactly the same as your competitors, and the only thing you can compete on is price, this Revolution may benefit your competitors more than it benefits you. You might still want to learn about it, though. Doing so will allow you to prepare, and perhaps rethink your strategy.

- **Geo-Local Offers** — The Audience Revolution is driven primarily by the geographic boundlessness of the online world. While some of these concepts will still hold for hyper-local businesses (i.e. dry cleaners, massotherapists, etc.), you may need to think a little further outside the box to see the fit and application.

- **Procurement via RFPs** — This refers to large corporate or government sales (usually in the five-, six-, or seven-figure price range), which are done through a "request for proposal" (RFP), and structured referral process. While the Audience Revolution can still buoy your chances, those processes are inherently designed to weed out the advantages offered by these strategies.

Before we dive into the nuts and bolts of these ideas, it always helps to start with a bit of context. Which, in this case, would be the plot twists that led me to this realization in the first place...

The Plot Twists That Led Me to the Audience Revolution

My entrepreneurial story began more than half a lifetime ago, when I quit school at fifteen to start my very first business. In the interest of expediency, though, I'll fast-forward to the timeframe of 2008-2010, which was the aftermath of my first "big" entrepreneurial venture.

The company was called MaestroReading. I set out to change the world by building software that would teach kids how to read — which I felt very passionate about then, and still do today. It was big in the sense of having raised some money, hired some people, built a prototype, and won some awards and accolades for innovative business thinking... but not big in the sense of actually having made any money. While I had done a good job of researching the problem of elementary reading, and building something that would help kids to learn, it never occurred to me to ask parents or teachers what they wanted or needed to help their kids. As a result, even though both kids and industry experts loved our software, the parents and teachers that would have been our actual customers never really understood the value of what we were doing. And while we might have had a chance to recover, we were hit by the kidney punch that was the market crash of 2008. The result: my company was down for the count, having achieved nothing but saddling me with a quarter of a million dollars of debt.

And as bad a situation as that may seem, you haven't heard the worst of it yet: while building MaestroReading, I had neglected my consulting practice. Not only did I have a quarter of a million dollars in debt, I also had no source of income to start paying it. So I did the only thing I felt I could do: buckle down, hit the pavement, and rebuild my practice. And it worked; within a couple of years I had built up to a fairly lucrative business, though not without some plot twists along the way.

My business "sweet spot" (i.e. the target market I could serve the best, and create the most value for) was small business owners in the 0-10 employee range — and closer to 0 than 10. In other words, businesses in the very early stage, who were just starting out and needed to see some traction. I found more than enough of them who could afford my services, and that was the bread and butter that drove the growth of my practice. However, I found even more businesses who weren't doing well at all; they needed a ton of help, but they couldn't afford to pay for it.

Having been in the same position so recently myself, I couldn't turn my back on them. I found myself giving a lot of my time away for free — which was fine and fair, considering how many people had gone out of their way to help and advise me when I needed it. That's how the entrepreneurial world works: you pay it forward. The problem was that my time couldn't scale; there was a very finite limit to the number of entrepreneurs I could help in this way.

I hit on a clever idea. I would build an online course to teach aspiring entrepreneurs everything I thought they needed to know. Now I didn't see it then, but in hindsight it's clear that I was repeating the same mistake I made with MaestroReading. After (correctly) identifying a problem in the market, I didn't ask anyone if my proposed solution was something they wanted or needed. I assumed that I knew best, and so I rushed ahead to invest thousands of hours (literally) building a massive training course that I "knew" they needed. It was the "Product First" approach that 99% of entrepreneurs follow, and it almost always leads to failure.

That's exactly what happened to me. The training program (which I called "Marketing That Works" — oh, the irony of hindsight!) never did well at all, and after trying to sell it for a couple of years with little result, I ended up pulling the plug on it. I've never done the math, but there's a good chance the dollars I made relative to the hours I spent on that project would make for the lowest wage I've earned in my lifetime.

Nonetheless, I'm grateful for that plot twist. Without it, I never would have learned the lessons that guided me to where I am today and allowed me to help thousands of others. The product never sold well, but trying to figure out how to sell it is what put me on the road to success.

Failure becomes Traction becomes Success

I started out like every other consultant, blogger, or coach who sets out to build a business online: reading the popular blogs, subscribing to the email lists of the experts of the day, and bouncing from shiny strategy to even newer and shinier strategy. I tried search engine optimization, social media, pay-per-click advertising, and all the rest of it... and just like most of my peers, I barely saw even a hint of success.

But I persisted. Never underestimate the importance of a strong work ethic in addition to solid strategies, because without the work ethic, you'll never get to the strategies that are solid! Finally, through a combination of missteps and serendipity, I stumbled onto the strategy of guest posting. It's is all about writing guest contributions for high-traffic blogs, which are published along with a by-line pointing back to you and your site.

After my first couple of guest post submissions — both of which landed articles on major sites, and both of which drove substantial traffic back to my own blog and business — I realized that this was a winning strategy (though I didn't fully understand why yet!) and threw myself into it. This all happened in 2011, and by the end of that year I had written over 80 guest posts for major blogs (in addition to another 40 or so on my own blog). This earned me the nickname "The Freddy Krueger of Blogging" (given to me by readers of my work, who commented that "it's like you're Freddy Krueger... wherever I turn, you're there!"). It did more than just attract traffic and exposure to my business and blog. For the first time, there was an audience of people following my work and listening to what I had to say.

As the audience slowly grew, I realized that it was my ace in the hole. I wasn't making much money from my business at the time, but what I did earn always came from those who had discovered my work online, followed my ideas, and subscribed to my email list to hear more about what I had to say. I hadn't yet fully understood the nuance or power of the Audience Revolution, but I did realize that as my audience grew, so too would my business. So I set out to grow it in the most strategic and intentional way that I could.

Because I was so focused on the outcome of growing my audience (as opposed to selling some product or service), it was natural for me to focus on what the audience actually wanted instead of what I thought they needed. The topic of "engagement" was hot at the time, but almost everything published seemed to assume you were a major business or brand with a giant following. In that case, your big challenge was to engage them more deeply. Hardly anything was available for those just starting out, and whose following consisted of three subscribers: themselves, their other email address, and their cat.

So I set out to create the book they all wanted to read, that would teach you how to build engagement even if you were starting from scratch. While I had ideas about how to solve this problem (having seen good results growing my own audience by this point), there were others whose perspectives would be more valuable. So I solicited the perspectives of dozens of experts and authorities on the topic.

Now, as an aside, I want to emphasize that this is NOT the sort of book I ever wanted to write. As a general rule, I hate compilation books — but this was the best answer to the questions that my audience (and the market at large) were asking. So I put my own biases aside and created the book that I knew people wanted to read.

The result was *Engagement from Scratch!*, and unlike my previous products, it was built to be what my audience wanted (and not what I thought they needed). I self-published it in November of 2011, and it became a runaway success. It has been downloaded over 100,000 times, has garnered hundreds of glowing reviews, and remained on the bestseller list for almost two years straight. My audience grew by leaps and bounds. As more people flocked to my work, more questions, comments, and feedback made their way into my inbox.

By far, the most frequently asked question I received was about how I managed to do so much writing. I was still doing a lot of guest posting at the time, and everyone wanted to know how I managed it; for a stretch of several months, I was getting 3-5 (unsolicited) emails per week asking me about it!

Now, I'd love to say that I quickly and savvily saw this for the opportunity that it was, and jumped on it...but that wasn't the case. The truth is that it took me months to notice the pattern, and months more before I stopped resisting (my focus still being on selling the doomed marketing training). But finally, after dozens of questions from my audience, I finally decided that if everybody wanted to learn how to do this, I would teach them. I tentatively offered a pilot program for this new offer, which I called "Write Like Freddy" (referring to my "Freddy Krueger of Blogging" moniker), and to my great surprise, it sold out almost immediately — faster than anything I had ever sold before.

I delivered the pilot and gathered feedback from my students, which I used to refine my curriculum and roll out an updated version of the product. The pilot was sold in January of 2012. By the end of that year, almost a thousand students had enrolled in my program. Write Like Freddy was my first blockbuster success.

The Secret of My Success was... the Audience!

It wasn't until several months later that I looked back on the successes that I had enjoyed with *Engagement from Scratch!* and Write Like Freddy that I realized the common thread they shared, and that made them different from the ill-fated MaestroReading and ironically named Marketing That Works: my failures followed the mainstream "product first, audience second" approach to business, whereas my successes were both created by placing the Audience First.

And in case you're wondering, these two projects weren't just lucky flukes. Since then I've launched two more blockbuster training programs and a number of other successful offers, following this Audience First philosophy and framework. Together they've grossed close to 3 million dollars in just a few years, and this is just the beginning. The best part is that not only do people happily buy our products, they also love us for creating and delivering them, because we're genuinely and excitedly making their lives better through our work with them.

This predictable growth grounded in sustainable and transformative impact isn't exceptional. On the contrary, it is the mainstay of the businesses that represent the first wave of the Audience Revolution: the new paradigm of business success that is sweeping the planet to create businesses that are more impactful, more profitable, and more rewarding to their creators. At the core of the Audience Revolution is a single, simple idea, that to be successful, and make an income by making an impact, you must do one thing: you must put the Audience First.

That's it: just put the Audience First. But it sounds so simple and straightforward! Surely, there's more nuance to truly understanding this idea? Yes, there is... so turn the page, and let's dive in!

All the Levels of Audience First

Over the course of my career, I've learned that while many strategies and tactics are effective in very specific contexts, there are very few principles of business that hold true in the majority of situations. Usually, if you try to take a business idea out of its element, it will be ineffective at best and downright damaging at worst. There are a few ideas, though, that have a fractal quality; they work in many contexts and at many different scales. They're rare, and when you find one, it's important to pay careful attention.

A good example of this sort of universal principle is the Pareto Principle, also known as the 80/20 Principle. Perhaps you're already familiar with it? It wouldn't surprise me if you are, because it's been written about by authors ranging from Vilfredo Pareto, who discovered it, to modern business authors like Richard Koch, Tim Ferriss, and many others. They all write about it because it applies to so many different contexts.

Another universal principle of business drives the Audience Revolution: that you must always put the Audience First. Do so and success will follow, regardless of whether you do it at the level of your business philosophy, your growth and execution strategies, or the specific tactics you employ. Let's explore what Audience First looks like at each of these levels of scale, and why it can be so impactful to your business.

Audience First as a Business Philosophy

Audience First as a philosophy is about putting the needs of your audience above all else, and seeking to be of service to them as much as is possible. As you read these words, you're probably doing two things, maybe even simultaneously:

1. Nodding in agreement, because the Audience First idea resonates on a deep level with our instinctive values and the Golden Rule: to treat others as we wish to be treatcd.

2. Raising an eyebrow at the feasibility of such an altruistic idea. This is understandable; after all, how can you make a profit if you're giving away the farm?

How to actually act on an Audience First stance is a very important question. The first step to answering it is to understand that we are not, in any way, shape, or form, talking about giving away the farm. Just as being a good parent doesn't mean letting your kids do whatever they want, serving your audience does not mean giving everything away for free.

Case in point: we give away a lot of information for free on our website, including substantial pieces of work that took a great deal of time and money to produce. We do it because we know that it benefits a lot of people, but that doesn't mean we give everything away for free. Our business makes money selling training courses that go deeper into the application and implementation of our Audience First ideas. These training programs are affordably priced, and great value for money, but they certainly aren't free. But, hypothetically speaking, why not give them away for free? Wouldn't that be better for the audience?

Actually, the answer is no, it wouldn't, for two important reasons: cost and commitment go hand in hand, and sales create sustainability of impact.

Cost and Commitment Go Hand in Hand

You may have been exposed to the idea that "people value what they pay for, and don't value what they get for free", and this is very true. More important than perceived value, though, is the question of how committed your customer will be. In the case of a free product, the answer is usually "not very committed" — and appropriately so. Free is a great price, not only because it doesn't cost us anything, but also because it doesn't commit us to anything, either.

As an example to illustrate this idea, imagine a new restaurant opening in your neighborhood. Let's say it's an Italian restaurant, and they're very motivated to make a successful go of it, so they're pulling out all the stops with their marketing. Now, the best way to get people excited about good food is to actually try the food. So they dispatch a waiter to stand outside the restaurant with a tray of gourmet mini-meatballs on toothpicks and offer them to passers-by. This is an excellent strategy; many passers-by happily take a meatball, taste it, and think about bringing their families and friends to this new restaurant.

But imagine if, instead of mini-meatballs on toothpicks, the restaurant set up a small table with a plate of fresh spaghetti and invited passers-by to sit down and eat. This wouldn't work nearly as well... but why not? On the face of it, they're giving away a lot more: an entire meal versus a single mini-meatball. Isn't that a "better offer?" We know it isn't. While passers-by can try the mini-meatball without changing any plans, the plate of spaghetti requires more of a commitment: the time to eat, and possibly the changing of their meal plans... not to mention solving a problem (being hungry) that might not even exist in the moment. Spaghetti is great, but only when you're ready to commit the time and appetite to sitting down and enjoying the meal!

This helps us understand where to draw the line between what we can (and often should) give away for free, versus what people should pay for. Anything that is quick and easy to "digest" is a good thing to give away for free; in my business that means articles, e-books, and short videos teaching big ideas that are relatively easy to grasp, or strategies and tactics that are easy to understand and implement. Those do a great job of serving my audience, demonstrating my expertise to them, and building my relationship with them by bringing them closer to their desired outcomes.

Some ideas take more effort to absorb and digest, though, and it isn't reasonable to give them to someone who hasn't committed to them. Our training programs teach strategies that are extremely powerful and effective, but they also require that our students invest time and work. Paying a fee is a signal to the self that "yes, this is something I've committed to", and that is a prerequisite for achieving worthwhile outcomes. A paying customer is a committed customer, and that's who you're best positioned to help.

The idea of cost and commitment going hand in hand really comes down to doing the best you can do for each individual member of your audience; each person who pays for your support is much more likely to take it seriously and benefit. But what about doing what's best for your audience as a whole?

Sales Create Sustainability of Impact

As idealistic and altruistic as our motives are, we must remember that any impact that matters will have to be made in one place: the real world. In the real world, we face constraints of time, money, and other resources, and the only way for us to make a real impact is to do it sustainably.

What does sustainability mean, especially in this context? It means that whatever impact you make must have a net positive effect on your ability to create further impact. In other words, helping one person doesn't deplete your time, money, or energy — it adds to them, creating the ultimate virtuous cycle.

(As a side note, I truly believe this is what business is really about. Not making money — although that can be a nice side benefit — but rather finding sustainable ways to accomplish whatever you want to accomplish, and make whatever impact you feel needs to be made).

So even if cost and commitment didn't go hand in hand (which they clearly do), would it create the greatest impact for me to give everything away for free? No, it wouldn't, because creating the best possible training courses, staying current on changes in the landscape, and offering the best possible support to our students all takes time... and doing it at scale takes money (because you have to hire more people to get it all done).

Starting this business as I did, with a quarter of a million dollars in debt, I could still have given everything away for free... but then my work would still be relegated to evenings and weekends alongside a day job that paid the bills. I would never have been able to reach the people I've reached or grow the organization I've grown. By charging a moderate fee for our training programs, we've been able to help thousands of people. Instead of just a few hours of my own time each week, I can devote the energy and focus of my entire organization (almost twenty of the smartest people I know) to supporting our audience in their goals.

This is true even if you have very deep pockets from the very first day. If your pursuits aren't financially sustainable, eventually you'll reach a point of scale at which your resources will run out, and this will necessarily curtail the impact you care about making. Sales and revenue allow you to create a sustainable impact, and that is the engine for true change in our world.

Now, to be clear, I'm not advocating that you charge more than you need. There's a big difference between charging fees that make your operation financially sustainable (and create proper commitment in your customers), and just gouging people. The former is in the best interest of your audience, and the latter most certainly isn't. It all comes down to what is truly in the best interest of each audience member *and* your audience as a whole; by charging a reasonable amount and running a good organization, you will be able to help many people in a very deep way, and you will grow your reach with free help for those who aren't as committed (yet).

That is the virtuous cycle of the Audience First philosophy when applied to your business. But in a practical sense, how does it tie into your strategies for execution and growth?

Audience First as a Growth and Execution Strategy

How do you start a business? Almost anyone asked this question (including many experienced entrepreneurs) will answer with some formulation of the following two steps: first think of something you can sell, and then find people who want to buy it. This "product first" approach to business is an implicit assumption so deeply ingrained that we don't even realize it's there until we say it out loud.

Product First is the paradigm of 99% of the business world, and it's the reason they all — from giant corporations to solopreneur coaches, consultants, bloggers, freelancers, authors, and change makers — find themselves on a treadmill of constantly having to find new customers. It's a frustrating rat race that causes many to go under, and creates cynicism and disillusionment for many more.

But what if there was an alternative that would allow you could break that cycle, once and for all? As you've probably already inferred from everything I've shared thus far, you can — by applying the Audience First approach to business that is driving the Audience Revolution. You do it, quite literally, by putting the Audience First: first you build the audience, and only then do you build the product (which, for our purposes, is anything you want to put out into the world in a financially sustainable and rewarding way, whether it's an e-book, a membership site, a training program, physical goods, services that you provide, a book that you want to write, etc.).

This procedure of building the audience before developing the offer has profound implications to the operation and growth of your business. For one, it bakes the ideas that drive the Audience Revolution right into the foundation of your business; rather than starting with an offer and then seeking to somehow "audiencify" your business, starting with the Audience First means that the audience will necessarily be your first point of reference.

It also means, counter-intuitively, that your audience (and therefore your business) will grow a lot faster if you aren't trying to hock your wares to them from the very first day. This is because people are inherently skeptical about the motives of the businesses around them — and who wouldn't be, given some of the scandals and abuses of the last several decades? Now of course, people understand that you are building a business and will ultimately have something to sell... but starting by offering ideas and value for free, as a starting point for attracting that foundational core of your audience, is a strong trust-builder and will accelerate the growth of your audience.

(Just to be clear, while it's better to build the audience before having a product or service, that doesn't mean that existing businesses are past saving. If you already have a business, or product, or website, but aren't where you want to be, simply "pretend" you're starting from scratch by building an audience in parallel with your regular business operations. Once the audience is in place, the two can tie together, and you'll be right back on a much better track).

To make this all happen, start by identifying the audience you want to serve and who are desperate for you to lead them. Then create a foundational online presence (which doesn't have to be elaborate; a simple page about who you are and what you are going to share, with an opportunity for visitors to give you a name and email address to receive more from you, is plenty!), and start driving traffic back to it.

And how do you drive that traffic? Simple. By going where the people you want to reach are already congregated: on blogs, in forums, and in social media groups. Share your ideas with them, with an invitation to learn more by visiting your site. This is precisely the strategy I stumbled onto, though I'm hardly the first, and I'll show you how this plays out for different businesses in the next section.

But before that, let's dig a little deeper into what the Audience Revolution looks like on a tactical level. Because strategy is great, and philosophy is even better, but at some point, we've all got to roll up our sleeves and start doing and selling things!

Audience First as Applied to Business Tactics

Let's assume for a moment that you not only understand, but also appreciate and are feeling deeply inspired by the Audience First approach to business that is driving the Audience Revolution. Let's assume further that you've committed to these ideas, and in the near future you will become the poster child of the Audience Revolution, with an engaging following of people who love your ideas and are excited to see what you'll share with them next.

This can happen quickly (if you follow the strategies laid out in this book and our training programs), or it can be a long and winding path filled with false starts and wrong turns (as it was for me when I stumbled onto these ideas for the first time). However you get there, though, once you're to the point of having an audience of true fans following your work, you still ultimately have to do what every business has to do in order to be sustainable: you have to sell something!

The mega-corporation approach to marketing and selling to an audience would be to treat it as any other channel, like television advertising or direct mail. Through whatever channel you access your audience (usually email, your blog, and social media, in that order), you communicate the message that "Hey, Audience Members, I've got something for you!" — and because you've worked hard to earn their trust and respect, and you deeply understand what matters to them, you'll probably enjoy pretty good results with this approach.

But really, that's simply the Product First approach transplanted onto the audience that you've built. And yes, the audience (being the silver bullet of business that it is) will multiply the results that you would otherwise experience — but if you apply an actual Audience First approach to your marketing and selling, the results can be so much better.

You do that by involving your audience deeply in the process of creating and marketing your offer. The term for this is "co-creation," and the idea therein is profound: it transforms someone from a passive prospect into an active partner by aligning your interests with theirs. Rather than announcing a new offer, you would share your idea (and the story of how it came to you from the audience) with your followers, and ask them if they want you to pursue it. This does more than just create a checkpoint for you to make sure you're on the right track; it also creates a true narrative that you're creating this offer specifically for them.

Then, with demand having been validated and interest formally expressed by your prospective buyers, don't let the energy dissipate as you retreat to your bat-cave to build a magnum opus of an offer. Instead, quickly turn around and offer a minimum viable version for immediate sale at a discounted price... but only for a limited number of charter customers, who promise to give you feedback on how you can make things even better.

That's what I did with Write Like Freddy, and every subsequent successful offer that I've made:

1. Listen to my audience to understand what they are telling me they want.

2. Reflect back to them what I am hearing, and ask if they truly want it.

3. Sell a discounted minimum viable version (usually a pilot course) to a charter group of students, who promise to provide feedback on how it could be made better.

4. Iterate through more pilots if necessary, until I get it just right.

5. Take everything I've learned and turn it into a full-scale product that goes on to massive success.

This is the Audience First approach to creating and marketing your products and services, and it works better than just about any other approach I've seen or tried, to the tune of...

- With Write Like Freddy in 2012, the first pilot offer created over $5,000 in revenue — not a big number by many standards, but for a side project that wasn't making any money yet, it felt like quite a windfall! The product then went on to attract over a thousand students and generate six-figures in its first year.

- With the Audience Business Masterclass in 2013, three successive pilots generated almost $80,000, all before our first big (multiple-six-figure) launch. Over the next couple of years, it went on to attract thousands of students and over a million dollars in revenue.

- And with the Course Builder's Laboratory in 2015, two pilots generated over $100,000 in revenue before the official launch, which then grossed just over a million dollars.

The Audience First approach has absolutely transformed my business, allowing us to grow from zero, nothing, and nobody, to a team of almost twenty people, multiple-seven-figures in revenue, and a massive impact on the lives of thousands of people. All of that is driven by our wonderful audience of bloggers, coaches, consultants, freelancers, authors, speakers, and changemakers.

And I'm not alone, or even exceptional. The Audience Revolution is transforming businesses in just about every niche and industry you can imagine. Let's continue, then, and explore how it's all happening for them, and how it might happen for you.

Reimagining Your Business Through Audience

While the Audience Revolution applies to virtually every niche, industry, and scale of business, people don't tend to learn well from generalities. We benefit most from specific contexts and examples that are directly relatable to our own realities. That is why, for the rest of this book, I will focus on the contexts and realities of the bloggers, coaches, consultants, authors, freelancers, and changemakers that I have the privilege of serving. These businesses are usually patterned on one (or several) of the following four basic structures:

1. **Selling Products** — Ranging from e-books, to membership sites, to training

courses, to physical goods, and even software.

2. **Selling Services** — From coaching, to consulting, to freelancing, to writing, to design.

3. **Writing and Publishing** — Whether it's fiction, non-fiction, intended for Kindle, paperback, or even a PDF e-book.

4. **Speaking and Training** — This includes speaking at conferences, keynoting, conducting trainings for corporations, and also consulting to c-suite executives.

These four business models all hinge on the knowledge, expertise, and passion of the entrepreneur, leveraging them to create a real impact on the world. Almost every one of the entrepreneurs I've served and trained fall into one of these four categories, and many have their fingers in more than one of these pots — in fact I've experienced success in all four, and this isn't uncommon with Audience First businesses, as you'll see.

So let's explore each of these four business models: what they looked like before the

Audience Revolution, how they have been transformed, and the impact that they have on businesses today, starting with the most common business model of them all: selling products.

The Audience Approach to Building and Selling Products

Selling products is the archetypal business model; we make something that people want and give it to them in exchange for a reasonable fee. The product is worth more to them than they have to spend to get it, and it costs you less to produce than they pay you for it. In other words, everybody wins. Or at least, that's how we imagine it's going to be before we set out to create our first product. Reality is messier, and often wracked with disillusionment and disappointment.

The more common path looks something like this: you get turned on to the idea that you can package up your knowledge and expertise in a way that will be usable and consumable by others, whether that takes the form of an e-book, a membership site, a training course, a physical solution of some kind, or even software. So you set to work, investing your blood, sweat, and tears (not to mention time, energy, and money!) into building this amazing product for the world.

It invariably takes longer than you initially expected; by the time it's done, you've probably invested months, or even years, to make it into what you know the market needs it to be. So you put the finishing touches on it, prepare your sales materials, flick the switch to make it all live, and... nothing happens. It's crickets. Tumbleweeds. Digital death.

Not knowing what could have gone wrong, you frantically search for the online marketing strategy or tactic you missed, the secret trigger to get your product to take off. You hear dazzling stories about gurus making millions of dollars in their underwear, and maybe you buy in (both ideologically and with your cold, hard cash) to their gimmicky strategies... but again and again, you find the emperor has no clothes and you've been left out in the cold.

When all is said and done, you feel defeated, frustrated, and disappointed. The product you've worked so hard to build — and that you knew could help so many people! — has been seen by less people than you can count on your hands (and several of them are friends and family who bought your product more to support you than because they actually wanted or needed it). No impact was made. No money was earned. And a great deal of time and energy was wasted.

Does this sound like a nightmare scenario to you? It is, but for many, it's a nightmare they live for months and years at a time. But the good news is that this tortuous experience is largely the result of Product First thinking, and as you've already learned, there's a better and easier way.

So how does this same business model look to those entrepreneurs who have embraced the Audience Revolution? It looks a whole lot better, for three key reasons:

1. **Your audience will tell you what they want.** Instead of basing the months and years of product creation effort on a hunch, it will be based on real-world

demand from people who already know what you're about and what you have to offer. More than anything else, this will help you build a product that people actually want, and they'll happy to buy it.

2. **Your audience will buy it before you create it.** Without an audience, you have little choice but to create something and hope for the best; this is not only risky, but also time-consuming and expensive, because you won't make any money until it's done. With an audience of loyal followers, you have the option of pre-selling your offer so that you get paid in advance. You'll have a budget to work with so that you can create something truly amazing.

3. **You will be selling from a position of trusted authority.** Your audience is comprised of people who know, like, and trust you, which means they will be infinitely more likely to buy from you. The real beauty is that having an audience of followers will help you sell

more effectively, even if you're dealing with complete strangers; the mere fact that other people trust you is enough to signal to newcomers that they should as well!

You've already heard my story of product creation with and without an audience. With MaestroReading and Marketing That Works, I built the product first and never got very far. With Write Like Freddy, the Audience Business Masterclass, and the Course Builder's Laboratory, I started with the audience first, made money well before the product even launched, and went on to impact the lives of thousands of customers.

Now, these are all great stories (particularly to me, since I got to live through them!), but they aren't unique or particularly special. Two other great examples (out of thousands I could choose from) are Copyblogger Media and Netflix.

Copyblogger Media started out as just Copyblogger, a blog about copywriting applied to blogging started by Brian Clark. He had nothing for sale, and gave a ton of great information away for free. The blogging world noticed, and started flocking to his block. His audience grew, and grew vocal. They told him what they liked (which was a lot), what could be improved, and very importantly, they also told him what they wanted. Brian listened, and created exactly the offer that they asked for, teaching exactly what they wanted to know... and the audience ate it up, to the tune of over a million dollars in sales in their first year selling anything!

That was only the beginning, though. The audience continued to grow, and Brian continued to listen. He created more products, and the business continued to grow — always driven by the loyal and engaged audience. A lot has changed since the early days of Copyblogger. Today, Copyblogger Media is the agglomeration of a handful of Brian Clark's partnerships, with most of the money coming from the sale of software products under the umbrella of their Rainmaker Platform product suite.

Now, how about an example a little further afield of our little world of blogging and online business? One of my favorite examples is Netflix and their hit show House of Cards. Even if you don't know (or like) the show, you probably know people who do... but did you know how intentionally the show was created based on knowledge of the Netflix audience? Everything about the show was engineered to be a success. Netflix has great data, after all, about the viewing patterns of its users; they know a large segment of their viewers likes political dramas and likes Kevin Spacey, and likes to binge-watch an entire season at a time. House of Cards was so successful because it was made to order based on what Netflix saw that their audience wanted!

Whether it's my business, or Copyblogger, or Netflix, or any one of thousands of other product-based businesses (including yours!), the unifying factor that drives great success is the simple act of building the Audience First, and seeking to serve them.

So clearly this works when building products ranging from online education products, to software, and even to online television! But what if you aren't selling a product at all? What if — like many coaches, consultants, freelancers, writers, designers, and online entrepreneurs — you're selling a service?

Who Better to Serve than a Leader?

A service business is the easiest business in the world to start. You don't need a product, you don't need to write a book, and you don't need to prepare a speech. All you need is something that you know or do better than someone who might try to do it for themselves. The services one might provide are endless, from business and life coaching, to specialized training and tutoring (on anything from math to college prep to bass guitar and everything in between), to consulting, to technical services like writing, design, or even accounting or law.

Whatever it is that you're skilled and passionate about, there are bound to be some people out there who have need of your expertise and would happily pay you for your services. And isn't that better than working a job you don't like, making too little money, all while creating business growth for someone else? Many aspiring entrepreneurs agree that it is, and so they build a website and hang up their shingle as a service professional ready to accept new clients.

Except that the clients don't seem to know, or care. The idea seemed so straight-forward and easy, but now you find yourself chasing fruitlessly after prospects at cocktail mixers and breakfast networking events that invite you to travel far from your home, pay an entrance fee, and make pointless small-talk with a dozen other entrepreneurs who care more about stuffing their business cards into your hands than hearing what you have to say.

The clients who end up doing business with you are few and far between, and they balk at fees that you know are much lower than they should be. In the end you find yourself with a handful of clients, feeling drained, and not making anywhere near the impact or income you originally set out to.

It's a depressing picture, to be sure, but it doesn't have to be this way. The incredibly common scenario I just described is a product of Product First thinking — and yes, you can still fall victim to it without even having a product to sell! By following an Audience First approach, things will look a whole lot better:

1. **Clients will come to you.** Whereas most service entrepreneurs are constantly pounding the pavement (both figuratively and literally) in search of new clients, you won't have to worry. Clients will find their way to you — after all, you're the authoritative expert who leads an engaged audience around your subject area, so who better to help them?

2. **Better and happier clients.** Unlike most service entrepreneurs, who have to explain their services and convince prospects that they need them, you're already a known quantity. The people who approach you will have been thinking about approaching you for quite some time, and they already know exactly why they need you.

3. **You can charge premium rates.** Since you're the authority, you're no longer competing with every other service provider out there. You're the expert,

in a whole different class from the competition, and the right clients will happily pay top dollar for your support and expertise.

This is exactly what I experienced in my own business. As I explained earlier, after MaestroReading I got back to consulting and was charging an hourly rate of $100/hour. Which isn't bad, except that I had to spend more hours than I care to remember in early morning networking meetings, handing out business cards, writing lengthy proposals, and even making cold calls! And to top it all off, some of my clients were far from "ideal."

When I set aside the business cards and networking breakfasts and focused on simply attracting and serving my audience, everything changed. My hourly rate has skyrocketed to $500/hour, and it's rare that I'll even accept hourly consultations; usually when I take on a consulting mandate it involves a multiple-five-figure fee just for a weekly phone call. And the best part is that I haven't handed out a business card in years; I don't attend networking events, or make cold calls, or submit proposals. More people approach me for consulting work than I have the bandwidth or inclination to take on, and when I do, they are willing and eager to pay my fees. Why? Because they already know, from having followed my work and seen me in action, that the results will more than justify what they pay.

And I'm not unique in this regard, or even the most impressive case study to illustrate the point. I'm not anywhere as expensive or sought after as celebrity consultants like Scott Stratten (who blogs at UnMarketing.com and wrote a great book by the same name) or Jim Collins (author of *Built to Last*, *Good to Great*, and other great books), both of whom followed the same basic approach: they built an audience by publishing their insights and ideas, and that audience in turn drives the demand for their services. Scott built his audience on social media, and Jim did it the "old fashioned" way, by publishing traditional books (because Jim got started in the 1990s, way before the words "social" and "media" ever meant anything together). But the basic pattern was the same: Audience First, and services second lead to a thriving, successful business.

Another example is Nir Eyal, who blogs at NirAndFar.com, and recently wrote a great book called *Hooked: How to Build Habit-Forming Products*. In addition to being a blogger and author, Nir is a sought after angel investor and advisor to startup companies in Silicon Valley. Now if you think about it, being an advisor to startups, and even being an investor, is a form of service. And how did Nir become so in demand? He started by publishing his ideas for free, and that attracted the audience that drove his book and practice to success. Which brings us to the third business model employed by many Audience Businesses: writing and publishing.

Authors Who Put the Audience First

I once heard a statistic that 80% of people aspire to write a book. That's four out of every five people! In other words, in a family of five, there's only one who doesn't want to write a book someday! Even if this seems like a high number, it speaks to an underlying truth of the human condition: we all have stories to share, and we all have ideas we want to gift to the world.

A generation ago, it was accepted that writing books was for "other people" — the authors who spent decades paying their dues with a mountain of unpublished manuscripts and rejection letters before the serendipitous discovery that turned them into an "overnight" sensation. After all, both *Harry Potter* and the *4-Hour Work Week* were famously turned down by dozens of publishers before someone agreed to give them a chance.

But today, things are different. We've all seen independent authors create massive successes; non-fiction examples include my friends Jeff Goins (author of *You Are a Writer*, *The In-Between*, *Wrecked*, and *The Art of Work*) and Sean Platt (author of more books than I can count, including *Write. Publish. Repeat.*), not to mention examples from the world of fiction, like E L James (*Fifty Shades of Grey*).

These successes light a fire in the imaginations of thousands of would-be writers. So finally, after much procrastination, they begin to write. And the writing process is longer and harder than they first expected it to be, but they persevere, keep on writing, and finally emerge with a finished manuscript: their pride and joy.

With a completed manuscript under their belts, something interesting happens: even though they may have been prompted to start writing by the idea of self-publishing, now that the manuscript is done, many begin to feel like it "deserves" a real, traditional publisher. Those who feel that way spend years poring through Writer's Market, submitting book proposal after book proposal, and approaching agent after agent.

All of which usually proves to be a dead end. So eventually they make their way back to the idea of self-publishing. This is easy enough; there are great resources about the whole process, by authors like Sean Platt (*Write. Publish. Repeat.*), Guy Kawasaki (*APE*), and many others. Those resources show you how to get your book up on Kindle, and even go the extra mile to get a paperback copy made with CreateSpace. You get it all done, and one day the book finally arrives, and you hold it in your hands for the very first time. It's a truly magical moment: you are an author!

Within a few days, though, the glow starts to fade as you realize that nobody is buying or reading your masterpiece. It turns out that just posting a book up on Kindle isn't enough; you actually have to do the work of spreading the word about it! So you cycle through a series of online marketing strategies (just like the hapless product-building entrepreneur that I described earlier), but to no avail; the unfortunate truth is that the vast majority of first-time authors sell less than 100 copies of their book.

Now, I know you can already see where this is going. If you start with the Audience First, things happen very, very differently. In fact, you may have noticed that a great deal of the examples I've shared of successful Audience Business leaders have all written books. Perhaps you were tempted to think that, "Sure, they have big audiences, it's because they're famous authors." But actually, they were able to become successful authors because they already had large audiences. With an audience to support you, the entire writing and publishing process looks completely different:

1. **Your audience will give you real-time feedback.** They will happily read sample chapters, give you feedback on ideas, or even serve as beta readers for entire drafts of the book. They know you and love you, and their feedback will help you guarantee that you're writing a future bestseller.

2. **You can access traditional publishing, and big advances.** These days, the name of the game for new author success is the platform you're bringing to the table. Publishing houses know this, and so the bigger your audience is, the more heavily they will court you with publishing deals and big (i.e. as high as six-figures or more) advances.

3. **You can make it a bestseller.** Whether you choose to self-publish or work with a traditional publisher, your audience will be there to buy and promote the book as soon as it is released (or, often,

before it ever goes live). They will help you to make the book a bestseller.

This is precisely what I experienced with my own book, *Engagement from Scratch!*. It was completely self-published and done on a very short timeline; it went from being an idea in my head to being available (digitally and in print) in just six months, which would be virtually impossible with a traditional publisher. This meant that the marketing and book promotion was entirely my responsibility, and yet the book was a great success.

It is important to note that, at that point in time, I hadn't yet built a very large audience. The day before the book was published, I had less than 1,000 subscribers on my email list. But in spite of the small size of my audience, and because of their enthusiasm and support, the book went on to do better than I ever thought possible: it has been downloaded over 100,000 times since publication, and it was one of the top 20 best-selling marketing books on Amazon for two years straight, with over 200 glowing reviews.

As impressive as this might be, it's a minor success compared to the thousands of other available examples. Consider Nir Eyal, the sought-after startup advisor and investor I introduced you to in the last section. His blog attracted an audience, and when he self-published *Hooked* it took off, achieving so much success that a traditional publisher took note and negotiated with Nir to re-publish it under their imprint.

Two more great examples are Jeff Walker (creator of the Product Launch Formula), and Jeff Goins (who you met earlier). They've followed the same pattern to launch massively successful books with the support of their audiences. Jeff Walker's first book, *Launch*, debuted in June of 2014 and skyrocketed straight to the top of the New York Times Best Sellers list, thanks to the support of his audience. Jeff Goins' books have all done extremely well for the same reason, and as I type these words he's gearing up to launch his latest book, *The Art of Work*. I've read a pre-release version, and I know the audience that Jeff has built up, so I'll personally be shocked if that one doesn't top at least some of the charts!

For another great illustration, let's turn to James Altucher, who is easily one of the world's most widely read bloggers. His opinions aren't always popular, but his fearless transparency and authenticity have attracted an audience of hundreds of thousands of regular readers. And he truly takes care of them; not only is James one of the more prolific authors on the web, but he invites audience interaction at every step in the process (he may be the only author I've seen actually publish his personal phone number on a blog and invite readers to call him with their problems!).

Fueled by his audience, James was able to independently release his 2013 book *Choose Yourself*, which took over Kindles all over the world and became #1 across several categories (business, investing, spirituality, and self-help).

Huge win, right? Well because of its wild success, and the fact that he had a legion of hundreds of thousands of rabid fans who would read literally anything he wrote, major publishers were obviously itching to get a piece of it. That's why for his next book, *The Power of No*, James and his co-author/wife Claudia had the luxury of choice, opting in the end to go with Hay House, one of the world's biggest self-help publishers.

And of course, we can't move past the topic of Audience First writing and publishing without some mention of Seth Godin. He is arguably the most influential marketer on the planet and has published dozens of bestsellers. For our purposes, though, the title that warrants the most attention is *The Icarus Deception*, which he published in 2012.

Even though the traditional publishing world has been very good to Seth, he decided to see if he could launch another bestseller on the strength of his audience alone. To do this he began a Kickstarter campaign with the modest goal of raising $40,000 to cover publication costs. With a single mention of the project to his fans, the goal was surpassed on the very first day. By the time the campaign closed, Seth had pre-sold thousands of books and collected nearly $300,000 in pre-sales.

Now, to be clear, none of these stories are about overnight success. Each and every one of these people worked long and hard to cultivate the trust and respect of a loyal and engaged audience. The point is that all of them were smart about it and built the Audience First… and you can do the same.

How Audiences Will Put You on the Stage

Picture this: an announcer's booming voice introduces you, and music begins to play as you run onto the stage. The spotlights are on you, so you can only make out the silhouettes of the thousands of people sitting in the audience, clapping their hands, and chanting your name. This experience isn't the exclusive domain of rock star musicians; top-tier speakers are greeted in much the same way, and they are paid handsomely every time they grace a stage.

Paid speaking is great work if you can get it, but getting it isn't easy. The traditional route to success in the speaking industry starts by scouring the requests for proposals (RFPs) published by major conferences. These are opportunities for anyone and everyone to apply to speak and explain why they and their topic are the best choice for the conference audience.

Except that most conferences are so inundated by applications that you'd most likely receive a form rejection letter ("We regret to inform you that due to an overabundance of qualified speakers...").

With enough persistence and effort, though, you will eventually break through and get noticed. When that happens you'll learn that new speakers aren't paid for their troubles; you'll be expected to pay your own way (hotel, airfare, etc.) to get to the conference. If you're lucky, you'll get a free ticket to attend the other sessions. And of course, as the newbie speaker, you'll get the worst time slot of the whole conference: on the second day, right after lunch, when half the audience is in a food coma and the other half isn't even in the room, because they're out networking!

If you stick with it, though, things do get better. The more you speak, the more opportunities there are for people to notice you. Some of those who notice you will invite you back, and that's when it really starts to click. The conferences start to proactively invite you, and when that happens they're a lot more willing to pay you for your time and effort. It's great once you get to the far end of this whole process, but getting there can be an expensive and exhausting multi-year slog. The entire process gets shortcut, though, if you already have an audience:

1. **They will approach you.** Since you're a recognized authority, your name on the speakers roster will draw attendees to the event. That means you don't have to apply — conferences will proactively approach and invite you to speak.

2. **They'll pay you, right from the beginning.** When conferences invite new or inexperienced speakers to present, there's always the risk they won't be any good; that's why they're unlikely to be paid. If you're a recognized leader in your industry, though, you're already a "known quantity" that can command a respectable fee.

3. **They'll pay for your travel and accommodations, too.** This would go without saying, except that most beginning speakers face the out-of-

pocket expense of hotels and airfare (not to mention having to take time off work if they're still in another job!).

I won't focus on my own story too much as an example here, because — of the four business models we're covering in this book — this is the business model that personally interests me the least, for two reasons. Firstly, I'm an introvert. I enjoy spending time with trusted colleagues in small groups, but the hordes of people that attend conferences are exhausting to me. And secondly, I'm a little strange in that I really don't like to travel. So in short, I just don't find the idea of getting on a plane and flying through multiple time zones to get on a stage in front of hundreds of people all that appealing.

Which is not to say that I never do it. I've spoken at major conferences like SES (Search Engine Strategies) and ICON (the InfusionSoft marketing conference), as well as at major universities including Yale and McGill. It's just not my bread and butter... so let's look at a couple of people for whom it is.

My two favorite examples of this are both friends of mine: Mitch Joel, and Randy Gage. Though they both happen to be tall and bald, they're otherwise very different personalities with very different messages. But they both followed the same basic process: start by building the Audience First, and let the audience serve as the springboard that gets you invited onto any stage you like. And the different ways speaking fits into their businesses are particularly fascinating.

For Randy, speaking has long been a big part of his business, and understandably so. When audiences love you so much that you get paid multiple-five-figures every time you get on a stage, there's a strong argument to keep on doing it! But Randy is smart enough not only to seize opportunity, but also to make the absolute most of it. When I met him, he had just recently come off of the success of his (then) most recent best-seller, *Risky is the New Safe*. The massive speaking tour was a big part of what had propelled this "business rock opera" (as he calls it) to success.

For Mitch, the appeal is very different. He also gets paid very handsomely to take the stage, but he doesn't do it for the immediate payoff so much as for the exposure and thought leadership that come along with it. It's that stature within the industry that has been key in attracting some of the most plum clients to his 150-person marketing agency, Twist Image, which was recently acquired by the world's largest marketing conglomerate WPP.

These are only two of the many ways that speaking might fit into your business strategy. The true beauty of speaking (as with writing and publishing books), is that an audience will empower you to do it — and at the same time, the act of doing it will help you reach and engage a larger audience. It's the ultimate virtuous circle that supports you and the people you work to help.

So now, all that remains is to ask... which audience will you lead?

Which Audience Will You Lead?

The very first step to joining the Audience Revolution is to find the audience you want to serve and who are waiting for you to lead them. This is, in fact, the biggest challenge faced by the bloggers, coaches, consultants, authors, freelancers, and changemakers I've trained: figuring out what audience you should be serving, and finding the passion of yours that will captivate and excite them.

Far too many people can't find a good solution to this problem, so they never even get started. And of those who do get started, the vast majority don't have the clarity they need about who they're looking to serve, and why those people need them. This means that right out of the gate they're doomed to a long and difficult road of spending lots of time and money on an endeavor that is unlikely to succeed.

In this section I'll teach you how to figure that out, using a few exercises that are drawn from inside our acclaimed Audience Business Masterclass training program. For a more thorough video explanation of these two exercises, and also worksheets you can use to complete them successfully, visit AudienceRevolutionBonus.com. There's no charge — the video and worksheets are my gift to you, in appreciation of you reading this far and being this committed to your business and the impact it will make on the world.

These exercises will show you how to find a subject you are passionate about, and through which you can help a lot of people with a problem or need that truly matters to them. Both of these elements are absolutely critical to your success.

If you choose a subject area you're truly passionate about, but that doesn't really solve a problem or create a delight for enough other people, it will never become more than a hobby. People who say you should just "follow your passion, and the money will come" are usually the people whose passions turned out to be really valuable to other people. The truth is that there are far too many people out there trying to build businesses around their passion without seeing any results. As much as they might care about the topic, there just isn't a viable market opportunity to support it — in other words, the passion you're writing and teaching about have to solve a serious problem or create a major delight for your audience, so that at least some of them would be willing and eager to pay you for those outcomes. Passion is important, but it isn't enough — there needs to be a strong market opportunity to tie into, otherwise your audience business will only ever be a hobby.

On the other hand, going after a viable business opportunity is critical, but it isn't enough. You must go after an opportunity that you feel deeply passionate about, for several reasons. For one, it's very hard to attract and serve a group of people when you don't really care about what you're talking about. But even more importantly, is the reality that in business (as in every other serious pursuit in life), results don't always come right away. Sooner or later, you're bound to hit a snag in the road. In Randy Pausch's book *The Last Lecture* he says that "the brick walls in the road aren't there to keep you out, they're there to keep everyone else out and give you a chance to prove how much you want it." If you aren't passionate about your work, you won't want it all that much, and you won't get past those challenges.

Exercise #1: Finding Your Passion

Imagine you've just won a very special contest, and as your prize you're going to get a year of paid vacation from work. to intensively study one subject. It can be any subject you like, but one of the rules is that once you start the year, you can't bail in the middle or switch topics. So you've got to be careful about what you choose. It shouldn't be a topic you're just curious about and don't have a lot of experience with, because you might find that you don't like it nearly as much as you think. It's important to choose something you already like and would look forward to delving deeply into.

With that scenario as a starting point, the exercise is to list five to ten subjects that you'd be willing and eager to spend a year studying. Don't worry about getting them in any kind of order — just write them down as they come to your mind. This exercise is a little harder than it initially sounds. It's easy to come up with the first two or three topics, and then you've really got to think about it. But it's really important that you do put in the extra effort to think of more topics, because the rest of this process will be a lot harder if there isn't much on the list.

That's the first exercise; a really effective trick for figuring out what subjects you're truly passionate about and have enough depth for you to dig deeply into and help others with. Because let's face it: if you weren't truly passionate about a topic, or it didn't have much depth, you wouldn't want to study it for a year!

Exercise #2: Finding Your Contribution

The second exercise is about finding topics where there's a viable market opportunity that you have the expertise to help people with. At different times in your life, different people have come to you for help, advice, support, and guidance. Through this exercise you'll explore those experiences and write them down, making a list of five to ten things people come to you for when they need help.

For this exercise, granular topics are better than general ones. If a broad subject area comes to mind, try to narrow it down or even break it into several sub-categories. So, for example, if your topic is "business" or "cooking," you might want to break it down into "online analytics" or "vegan baking."

A common concern people raise when I talk about this exercise is that they aren't real experts on these topics. If that's your concern, don't worry — expertise is relative. What do I mean by that? Well, for every topic, there are all different levels of experts, just like there are different levels of teachers. Take math as an example. There are teachers who teach math at the elementary school level, the high school level, the college level, the graduate level, and the post-graduate level. Those are very different levels of knowledge and skill, and obviously most elementary school math teachers don't have the knowledge to teach math at the post-graduate level! That's the analogy most people think of when they feel like they aren't "expert enough" to teach something. They equate themselves to someone who could teach elementary school math, but feel like that person isn't a "real expert."

Here's the problem with that thinking, though: while it's true that most elementary school math teachers can't teach math at the post-graduate level, it's also true that most people who teach post-graduate math probably wouldn't be good at teaching elementary school, even if they do have the math knowledge! The truth is that being a good teacher — or consultant, or coach, or speaker — has even more to do with knowing your student than it does with knowing the subject matter. That's why, for a second grader who struggles, sometimes the best tutor is the fourth grader who has just recently mastered the same material. They know what it's like to struggle with it, and they know the tricks that helped them to understand it. Because the learning process is still fresh in their minds, they understand what the second grader is going through in a way that even the elementary school teacher just can't.

So don't worry about not being expert enough. If it's a topic on which people come to you for help, that means you know enough about it to help other people. So write those down on the second worksheet! And as you're doing that, make sure not to gloss over the things people come to you for that seem easy to solve, or "no big deal." Actually, when something is difficult for other people but easy for you, that's often a clue that a special unique ability of yours might be hiding beneath the surface, just waiting for you to seize it.

Putting it All Together

Once you've completed both exercises, the next step is to put both lists next to each other, side by side, and look for the things that show up on both lists. Sometimes the fit will be strikingly obvious — you may have even used the same words on both of the worksheets. Other times the fit isn't quite as obvious, but trust me, it's there — you just have to look where the lists might intersect to find it. Go through the list and look for the ways the topics you love might be connected to the things people ask you for help with.

This is the starting point for long-term success in the Audience Revolution: the intersection between your passion and the real market opportunities it can fulfill. And remember, for more detailed video training about these two exercises, complete with downloadable worksheets, visit AudienceRevolutionBonus. com. It's completely free; the training and worksheets are my gift to you, in appreciation of your reading this far and being this committed to your business and the impact that it will make on the world.

Can We Call This Your "Plot Twist"?

Since starting my business in 2011, I've shared this message of the Audience Revolution with tens of thousands of aspiring entrepreneurs. In doing so I've seen a pattern of common reactions I've learned to expect.

For many, these ideas represent a breath of fresh air. These aspiring online entrepreneurs already had an inkling that great opportunity for income and impact existed, but their pursuits hadn't been fruitful. Most likely they'd gone after a few shiny new strategies taught by "internet marketers." You know the kind I'm talking about; they're the ones preaching the exploitation of whatever platform and loophole *du jour* will supposedly allow you to make a quick buck. But those strategies and tactics haven't worked, and the snake-oil has left a bitter taste in their mouths.

When these entrepreneurs come to us, it's because they intuitively grasp that the Audience First approach is built on a stable foundation. They don't need a "guru" to sell them on it — it just makes sense that if you attract and serve an audience, all the good things I described in this book will follow. This approach to business resonates with their values and allows them to pursue a better future with heads held high.

For others the inspiration is mixed with frustration, and sometimes even a sense of profound defeat. After all, the time and money spent chasing fruitlessly after those other strategies weren't trivial. And now, years and many thousands of dollars later, it's difficult to accept that so much of it might have been for naught.

If that's the way you feel right now, I want to remind you that failure is only failure if it happens in the last chapter. Otherwise, it's a plot twist. So if that's where you are right now — feeling defeated by the realization that you've been going about this all wrong — then let this be your plot twist that leads to something much bigger and better.

Because even if you feel a little behind right now after reading the success stories I've just shared with you, remember that we're only at the beginning of the sea change that the Audience Revolution is bringing to our economy. It isn't too late for you to get out in front of it and win big by helping the people you care most about serving. Don't let yesterday's ideas constrain your imagination for a better and brighter future.

The real question to ask yourself is whether all this resonates with you. Do you feel lit up by the idea of making an income by making an impact, sharing your knowledge with the world, and truly putting your Audience First?

I hope you do, and I hope this book has been the push to get you started building a business that is sustainable and impactful to you and to those you will serve.

Audience Revolution Resources

Any time you need more help, training, or information about how you can leverage the ideas that drive the Audience Revolution, you're invited to explore the following resources:

Which Audience Will You Lead? A Crash Course in Finding the Niche that Needs You, and that You're Excited to Serve

We assembled this free video training course to guide you through the exercises in the "Which Audience Will You Lead?" section of this book. The training includes examples and worksheets you can use and apply to find your own passion, contribution, and the intersection where the greatest opportunity lies. There's no charge; the video and worksheets are my gift to you, in appreciation of your reading this far and being this committed to your business and the impact that it will make on the world.

Go get it right now at AudienceRevolutionBonus.com.

The Audience Business Masterclass: A Step-by-Step Framework, with Tons of Support

The critically acclaimed Audience Business Masterclass has guided thousands of students to build their own Audience First businesses. Through the program, you'll learn:

- How to lay the foundation that will drive your blog and business to success,

- How to create real relationships with major authorities in your space,

- How to launch explosively to massive excitement and success, and

- How to launch truly profitable offers doing the work you're really excited to be doing.

For more details, and to join the program, visit AudienceBiz.com.

The Firepole Marketing Blog and Resources

Firepole Marketing is one of the top marketing blogs in the world. On the site you'll find over 700 free articles and 100 free podcast interviews, and when you register for a free membership you'll also get dozens of e-books, video trainings, and Danny's entire first bestseller, *Engagement from Scratch!*.

Go explore the site and register for your bonuses at FirepoleMarketing.com.

Need In-Depth Business and Marketing Help? You Can Borrow Danny's Brain

Has your online business stalled? Are you having trouble attracting traffic, subscribers, or sales?

Danny has helped thousands of entrepreneurs overcome these (and many other) online business problems. If you're facing a business challenge that has you stumped, a single session with Danny may be the solution.

Danny does full-scale mentoring with only a select number of clients due to time constraints, but he does occasionally have availability for one-time Borrow My Brain sessions. For details, visit FirepoleMarketing.com/coaching-consulting.

About Danny Iny

In 2011, Danny founded a small blog called Firepole Marketing. Over the last few years he's grown it into a multiple-seven-figure authority in the industry with a team of almost twenty people, serving a community of tens of thousands of online entrepreneurs. In the process, he wrote the Amazon bestseller *Engagement from Scratch!* and created blockbuster online marketing courses including the Audience Business Masterclass and the Course Builder's Laboratory. He lives in Montreal, Canada with his wonderful wife (and business partner) Bhoomi and their soon-to-be-born daughter.

Danny is a super-friendly guy who makes a point of responding to his emails and messages within 24 hours — so follow him on Twitter @DannyIny, or just send him an email (danny@firepolemarketing.com) and say hello!

Made in the USA
San Bernardino, CA
24 February 2018